GEOGRAPHY DETECTIVE

Islands

Philip Steele

 Carolrhoda Books, Inc. / Minneapolis

All words that appear in **bold** are explained in the glossary that starts on page 30.

Photographs courtesy of: Aeroservice/Science Photo Library 8; The Hutchison Library / John Downman 19t; / John Hatt 23t; Impact Photos / Paul Forster 11t; Robin Taylor 25; Robert Harding Picture Library 13; South American Pictures / Tony Morrison - title page, 9, 18; / Peter Ryley 22, 23b; Sygma / P. Vauthey 14t; / Haruyoshi Yamaguchi 19b; Zefa - 4, 5t & b, 6, 7, 10, 11b, 14b, 15t & b, 16, 17, 20, 21t & b, 26, 27.

Illustrations by David Hogg. Maps by Gecko Limited.

This edition first published in the United States in 1996 by Carolrhoda Books, Inc.

All U.S. rights reserved. No part of this book may be reproduced, stored in a retrieval system, or transmitted in any form or by any means, electronic, mechanical, photocopying, recording, or otherwise, without the prior written permission of Carolrhoda Books, Inc., except for the inclusion of brief quotations in an acknowledged review.

A ZOË BOOK

Copyright © 1995 Zoë Books Limited. Originally produced in 1995 by Zoë Books Limited, Winchester, England.

Carolrhoda Books, Inc., c/o The Lerner Group
241 First Avenue North, Minneapolis, MN 55401

Library of Congress Cataloging-in-Publication Data

Steele, Philip, 1948-
   Islands / Philip Steele; [illustrations by David Hogg; maps by Gecko Limited].
     p. cm. — (Geography Detective)
   "A Zoë book" — T.p. verso.
   Includes index.
   Summary: Text and illustrations, with questions and activities, describe the formation of and life on islands around the world.
   ISBN 0-87614-997-2
     1. Islands — Juvenile literature. [1. Islands.] I. Hogg, David, 1943- ill. II. Gecko Ltd. III. Title. IV. Series.
GB471.S72 1996
551.4'2 — dc20   95-18276
                                                              CIP
                                                              AC

Printed in Italy by Grafedit SpA.
Bound in the United States of America
1 2 3 4 5 6 01 00 99 98 97 96

Contents

Exploring Islands	4
Cut Off by Water	6
Islands that Grow	8
Islands in Rivers and Lakes	10
Restless Continents	12
Islands of Fire	14
Islands of Coral	16
Artificial Islands	18
Islands and Plants	20
Island Wildlife	22
Living on Remote Islands	24
Islands and Global Warming	26
Mapwork	28
Glossary	30
Index	32

Exploring Islands

An island is a piece of land that has water all around it. Islands form in many different ways and vary in size. Some islands may be very large, while others are just small pieces of rock. Islands may be whole countries or small areas where no people live.

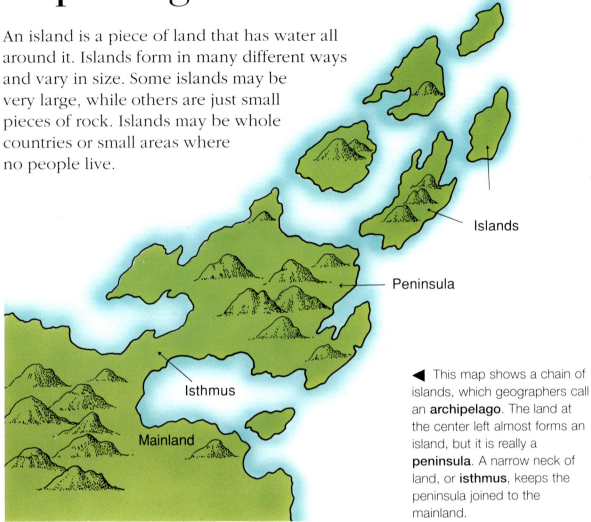

◀ This map shows a chain of islands, which geographers call an **archipelago**. The land at the center left almost forms an island, but it is really a **peninsula**. A narrow neck of land, or **isthmus**, keeps the peninsula joined to the mainland.

▶ This picture of Australia was taken from a satellite. Although surrounded by water, Australia is so huge that it is usually described as a continent rather than as an island. Around Australia's coast are smaller islands, such as Fraser Island, Melville Island, and Tasmania.

▶ Spirit Island lies in Maligne Lake in western Alberta, Canada. The lake and island are part of Jasper National Park.

● Greenland, the largest island that is not a continent, occupies an area of about 839,768 square miles in the Arctic Ocean. A thick layer of ice covers Greenland. Beneath the ice may lie several smaller islands.

● Indonesia, in Southeast Asia, has almost 14,000 islands — more than any other country. There are five main islands and 30 archipelagos.

Most islands are found in the oceans and seas, but some are in lakes and rivers. Sea islands can be hundreds of miles from the nearest large piece of land, or mainland. However, most sea islands are close to the coasts of larger islands or continents. In very cold areas, such as the Arctic and the Antarctic, islands may be joined to one another by sheets of ice or frozen seas.

Birds, animals, and plants can live on most islands. But people need a supply of fresh water and enough soil to grow food if they are to survive on islands.

Geography Detective

The island of Mont St. Michel lies off the northwestern coast of France. At one time, people could walk to the island only at low tide. Today a raised road, or causeway, links the island to the mainland.

How do people reach islands? Explain why people use different types of transport, such as boats, planes, or helicopters. When is it possible to build bridges or tunnels?

Cut Off by Water

Sometimes the mainland sticks out into the sea, shaping a **headland**. Over a long period of time, waves wear away, or **erode**, the rocks of the headland. The waves carve out caves and arches. When an arch or an isthmus collapses, a small island called a **stack** forms. A narrow channel of water may separate the stack from the mainland.

▲ Waves off Cannon Beach, Oregon, have pounded and eroded stacks of jagged rock.

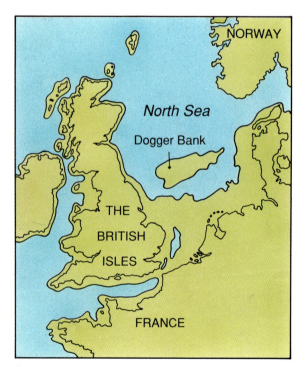

▼ The seabed of the channel between Britain and France is made up of layers of clay, chalk, and marl. These layers of rock stretch unbroken between the two countries. Before the English Channel formed, Britain was part of continental Europe. A new rail tunnel that runs through the seabed links France and Britain again.

▲ About 10,000 years ago, an **ice age** was ending. As the ice melted, water flooded large areas of northern Europe. The sea created what is now the English Channel, and Britain became an island. Before that time, Britain had been part of the European mainland.

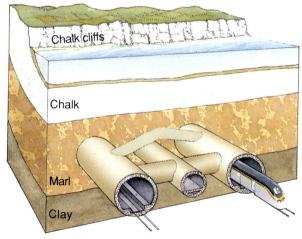

▶ Over the ages, the levels of the world's oceans have risen and fallen many times. New Guinea was once joined to Australia, and the islands of Sumatra, Borneo, and Java were once part of the Southeast Asian mainland.

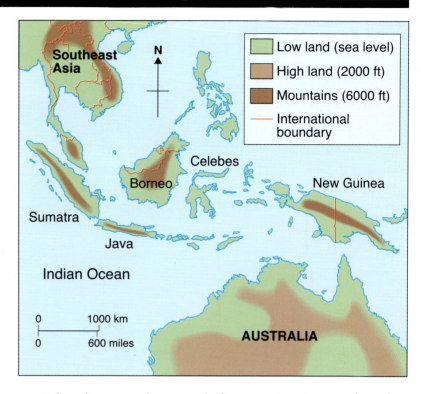

● During some ice ages, the sea sank 328 feet below today's levels. Many islands were then joined to the nearest landmass. Early humans settled these regions but were cut off when sea levels rose again.

Islands may also result from a rise in **sea level**. Low-lying land is flooded, but hills and high ground are left sticking up out of the water. These high places become islands.

Geography Detective

This rocky headland, once part of the coastline of southeastern Australia, was called London Bridge because the sea had broken through the rocks to form arches. In 1990 the arch nearest the land collapsed, forming a new island. Draw a picture of how you think the bridge might look today.

Islands that Grow

Some islands are created when land rises from the seabed. Over thousands of years, water currents may leave, or deposit, mud, sand, or shells in certain places. Waves may pile up these materials into banks that rise above the waves.

Soon plants seed themselves on the banks. Their roots spread out, trapping even more mud and sand. Leaves fall and rot to make new soil.

▼ The Colorado River flows for 1,488 miles from the Rocky Mountains into Mexico's Gulf of California. On the way to the Gulf, the river picks up soil, or **sediment**. This photograph was taken from the air and shows where the river enters the Gulf. The image has been specially colored to show how the sediment is deposited at the river's mouth to form a **delta**, which splits the river into a maze of smaller channels. Small islands form between the channels.

▶ The Chincha Islands lie off the coast of Peru, South America. Over time, they have been covered with the droppings, or guano, of birds, such as cormorants, pelicans, and boobies. The guano builds up in layers that can be many feet thick.

● The largest island in any delta is Marajó Island in Brazil. Lying in the Amazon River, Marajó covers an area of 18,533 square miles.

● The Pacific island of Nauru once had huge deposits of guano that were mined for use as fertilizers. The mining of guano brought wealth to residents but also destroyed the island's natural landscape.

Birds may nest on the ground, leaving behind layers of droppings, or **guano**. The buildup, or **accretion**, of sediment, wind-blown soil, and guano may increase the size of an island.

Geography Detective

Sediment may be made up of the remains of minerals, plants, or animals. Can you think of any animals that would leave behind shells? Which ones would leave behind bones? What would happen when these materials were pounded by ocean waves? Where would you see deposits like these?

Islands in Rivers and Lakes

When rivers wear away a valley, sometimes a piece, or **outcrop**, of hard rock is not fully eroded. Water flows around it, and the outcrop becomes an island. As rivers travel across a plain, they may divide and join again, leaving some dry land between the channels of water. Islands that form in this way may be very large. Brazil's Bananal Island lies in the Araguaia River, and has an area of 6,988 square miles. As the course of a river winds, its bends, or **meanders**, may also cut off areas of dry land.

▼ The Norman River is in Queensland, Australia. After leaving the Eastern Highlands, it winds across a plain. Bends in the river have created small islands.

► The currents in a river may create a braidlike pattern of islands in a riverbed.

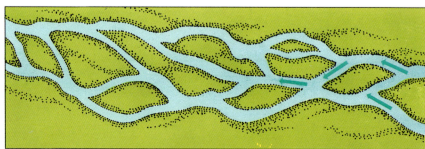

▶ Rainy Lake, Voyageurs National Park, Minnesota

● The biggest lake island is Manitoulin, which has an area of 1,068 square miles. Manitoulin lies in the Canadian part of Lake Huron.

Northern lands such as Finland and Canada bear the scars of the last Ice Age. The landscape is pitted and gouged by ancient movements of the ice. The holes and cracks in the land later flooded and became lakes. Higher land was cut off by the water. Maps show thousands of small islands and lakes.

Geography Detective

River islands are often settled and built over. They can be linked to the river's banks by bridges. The following big cities are built over river islands: Paris (right), New York City, Montreal, and St. Petersburg. Use an atlas to find out where these cities are. What rivers are they on?

Restless Continents

The rock that makes up the earth's surface is called the **crust**. It floats on a bed of semi-molten rock and is cracked in places, like a gigantic eggshell. Each cracked section of the crust is called a **plate**.

The plates do not stay still, no matter how solid the ground beneath may feel. They move very slowly. Over millions of years, these great movements in the earth's crust push continents together or pull them apart. In this way, landmasses may be surrounded by the ocean. The water may form new island continents.

● In the future, California may become an island. India, too, together with Southeast Asia, may form a new island continent.

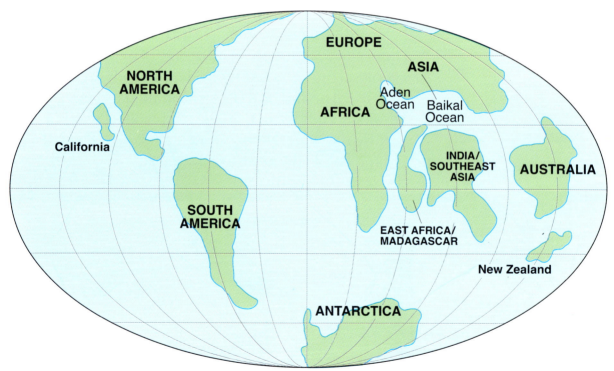

The coasts of continents do not always plunge straight into deep water. In many places, a ledge of land called a **continental shelf** stretches out from the coastline. Shallow seas cover the shelf, whose higher parts may rise above the waves to form islands.

▲ Computers can predict how the earth's continents will move in the future. This map shows how the world may look 50 million years from now. Some of today's large landmasses may split up to form new islands. Other landmasses may merge to make new continents.

◀ The island of Newfoundland, Canada, rests on the continental shelf that runs down the eastern edge of the North American continent.

Geography Detective

The movements of the earth's crust can push up rock. Land that was once part of the ocean floor can become high continental mountains. How do we know this? One way is to look for the remains, or **fossils**, of creatures that lived millions of years ago. They have been pressed into rocks that may now be thousands of miles from the sea. Look at the fossil in the picture. From what kind of creature was it formed?

Islands of Fire

◀ Surtsey is an island off the coast of Iceland in the North Atlantic Ocean. In the 1960s, hot magma bubbled up from the seabed to create Surtsey. As the island cooled, great clouds of steam rose from the sea.

Molten rock from deep inside the earth is called **magma**. It bursts through weak points in the earth's crust, producing **volcanoes**. The magma also oozes through parts of the ocean floor where plates are slowly moving apart. The red-hot liquid rock cools in the sea water.

Over long periods, the cooled magma builds up into high underwater ridges and cones. These shape underwater mountain ranges. Their peaks may rise above the surface to form new islands.

◀ The Hawaiian Islands in the Pacific Ocean are the peaks of massive underwater mountains that formed from cooled magma. Some of Hawaii's mountains are volcanoes that are still active. When Kilauea erupted in 1983, for example, great spurts of fire and bubbling rock flew into the air.

Case Study

Most volcanic islands are found in oceans, but they can exist in freshwater lakes as well. Crater Lake in Oregon, the deepest lake in the United States, plunges 1,932 feet into the heart of a volcano.

The volcano was already ancient when it erupted in a great blast 6,800 years ago. When that happened, its peak collapsed inward, forming a **caldera**. Since then, this five-mile-wide crater has been filling with rain and melting snow.

Recently, though, volcanic activity began building up a new cone of **lava** at the bottom of Crater Lake. The lava eventually rose above the blue waters of the lake, forming Wizard Island.

◀ Wizard Island in Crater Lake

Geography Detective

Heimaey is a volcanic island near Iceland. In January 1973, its active volcano erupted, spewing up lava and black ash. The islanders managed to escape, but many of their houses were badly damaged. Try to find out more about the eruption on Heimaey. How do you think the people escaped? What sort of damage would the eruption have caused?

Islands of Coral

◀ Coral islands are best viewed under water. Equipped with a snorkel, a mask, and flippers, people can swim to corals, where they will also see beautiful fish, seaweed, and shellfish.

Tiny creatures called **corals** are found mostly in warm, tropical seas. Corals have soft bodies inside a chalky skeleton. Many corals live and feed together in large groups. When the corals die, the soft part decays, and the skeleton remains. As new corals grow and die, the mass of skeletons builds up and hardens. The collected skeletons may reach the surface of the sea to form a coral **reef** or rise even higher to create an island.

Corals often collect around volcanic islands. Sometimes old volcanoes sink back into the sea or are swamped by rising seas. The corals keep multiplying until they form a ring around the place where the volcano used to be. These ring-shaped islands or archipelagos are called **atolls**. The calm water inside an atoll is called a **lagoon**.

▶ A great ledge of coral reefs surrounds Moorea, one of the Society Islands in the South Pacific Ocean.

● The widest coral ring made by an atoll is Kwajalein in the Marshall Islands of the western Pacific Ocean. The lagoon in the center of the atoll has an area of 1,100 square miles.

● Australia's Great Barrier Reef, the world's biggest reef, is more than 1,243 miles long.

▼ These diagrams show how atolls are formed.

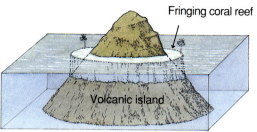

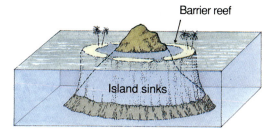

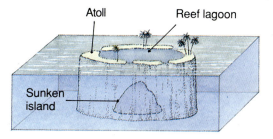
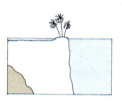

Geography Detective

Many corals are in danger. Some are eaten by a type of starfish called the Crown of Thorns. People collect corals for jewellery or for souvenirs. Sewage and oil spills encourage small plants called **algae** to grow instead of the corals.

Corals are also threatened by oil drilling, by dredging, and by the hot water that power stations pump into the sea. What do you think should be done to protect coral islands and reefs? What laws might be passed?

Artificial Islands

Not all islands form naturally. Long ago, people found that if they lived on islands in lakes they could defend their dwellings from enemy attack. Ancient lake villages in Switzerland were built on platforms that rested on wooden pillars. In Ireland and Scotland, early settlers created islands called **crannogs** in shallow lake beds using timber, stones, brushwood, and heather.

▲ The Aztecs lived in Mexico about 500 years ago. This painting by the Mexican artist Diego Rivera shows the great Aztec city of Tenochtitlán, which the people set up on an island in a shallow lake. The Aztecs built artificial islands around the city with mud from the lake. Workers held down the mud with poles and reed mats. Then the Aztecs planted trees around the islands' edges. The people found that the lake's rich mud was ideal for growing crops.

▶ Humans are not the only ones to make artificial islands. The beavers of North America build dams and lake dwellings, or lodges, with twigs, branches, and mud — materials that freeze solid in winter.

● A barrier in Britain's Thames River created nine mini-islands in 1984. The new islands are concrete bases that support flood-control gates. The gates can be raised if a high tide or a storm threatens London, Britain's capital.

Lagoons also provide a good base for artificial islands. In the shallow waters of the Pacific, the Lau people of Malaita in the Solomon Islands pile up rocks on top of which they build their homes.

Today engineers make artificial islands of toughened concrete. Concrete can carry heavy loads and resists erosion. Small concrete islands may bear the weight of the uprights of big bridges. They may also support the emergency barriers that protect cities against flooding.

Geography Detective

Airport runways are sometimes made on platforms above the sea. The runway shown here — Kansai Airport near Osaka, Japan — opened in September 1994.

Some people have suggested that in the future most airports should be built offshore on huge artificial islands. Why do you think this might be a good idea? What problems might occur?

Islands and Plants

◀ The coconut palm is perfectly adapted to life on tropical islands. It sprouts even in salty coastal soils. The trunk of the full-grown tree is strong, yet it can bend easily during hurricanes.

▼ The big fruit floats from one island beach to another. Its seed, the coconut, is protected by a tough fiber casing.

Islands may be thousands of miles from the nearest land. Surrounded by the empty ocean, they are often battered by gales, hurricanes, or **monsoons**. Yet many islands are covered in a rich carpet of plants, and some of the plants are not found anywhere else on earth. How did the plants get there?

Winds carry many seeds to islands. Some plants produce very light seeds that can float thousands of feet above the earth. These may drift down to an island by chance.

Birds that visit islands may have tiny seeds clinging to their feathers. In their droppings, the animals may also leave behind the seeds of berries that they have eaten. Other plants may have seed pods or nuts that are washed up on island beaches, where the seeds may take root and sprout.

Islands that were created by flooding or by erosion may have kept the plant life that they had before they were cut off by the sea. Madagascar, a large island that has long been separated from Africa's eastern coast, holds many unusual plants. Islands that have never been connected to a mainland can also develop unique kinds of plants.

● In August 1883, a massive volcanic eruption blew up Krakatoa, an island in Indonesia. Only parts of the island survived, and for a time nothing could live there. Yet within only 14 years, 61 types of plants had reappeared.

● The rosy periwinkle plant lives on Madagascar in the Indian Ocean. The plant's leaves provide a medicine for a blood disease called leukemia.

◀ Mangroves are trees that take over, or **colonize**, muddy shores in the tropics. The trees' long, tangled roots trap mud and any other materials carried by the sea. In this way, an island's shores can expand.

▼ Many plants in the Pacific nation of New Zealand, such as these red-flowering rata vines in the center, are found nowhere else in the world.

Geography Detective

Tropical islands, because of their moist climate, often have a wide variety of unusual plants. Choose a tropical island and find five plants that grow there and nowhere else. Find out if the plants are in danger of dying out. What do you think could be done to save your island's plant life?

Island Wildlife

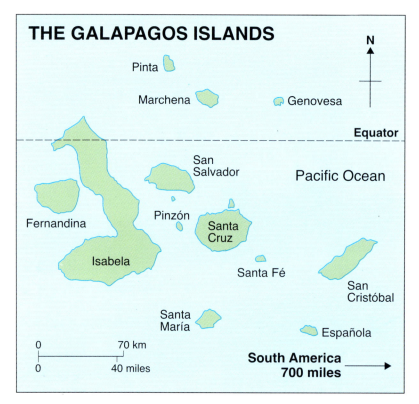

◀ All kinds of unusual creatures developed on the Galápagos Islands, far from South America's Pacific coast. The first finches to colonize the island, for example, developed into 15 different species, all of which ate different foods.

▼ The word *galápagos* means "tortoise" in Spanish. Fourteen different types of giant tortoise once lived on the islands. Sailors hunted the tortoises for food until many types died out completely, or became **extinct**. Many of those that are not extinct are **endangered**, meaning that they may yet die out because there are so few of them left.

Flying insects and birds can easily colonize new islands. Snakes and rats may float from one island to another on rafts of weed or storm debris. If islands are near the coast, wild animals from the mainland may swim out to them. In East Africa, even elephants have been known to do this.

Most oceanic islands have many marine creatures. Coasts not only provide breeding places for seabirds, they are also resting places for birds that travel, or migrate, over long distances.

Remote islands, where humans do not often visit, can be home to seals, sealions, or various types of bears.

Wildlife cannot easily escape from an island. If the wildlife on remote islands has never met any enemies, the arrival of humans or non-native animals can be a disaster. People may bring in cats and dogs that kill wild creatures. Settlers may cut down the forests where the wild animals live.

- Madagascar holds many unique kinds of wildlife. The lemur, for example, is a monkeylike animal that lives mostly in trees.
- Kodiak Island, off the coast of Alaska, is a safe place, or **refuge**, for Kodiak bears — the biggest meat-eating creatures in the world. The island also has a thriving salmon industry and is home to rare bald eagles and migrating seabirds.

▼ The fiercest looking creature on the Galápagos Islands is a harmless reptile, the marine iguana. It eats seaweed and likes to bask in the sun.

▲ The rare Galápagos hawk was not afraid of people. Many of these hawks were killed by the first human settlers.

Geography Detective

The Caribbean Sea is deep and is often swept by hurricanes. Birds and small animals, such as lizards, have colonized many Caribbean islands. These same species also live in Central and South America. How do you think these species might have reached the islands? Why do you think that the large mammals of North and South America are not found on the islands?

Living on Remote Islands

People live on islands for all kinds of reasons. Islands have been easy to defend from attack. They are rich in food, such as fish and shellfish. Many islands have sheltered harbors that make good bases for trading.

Island climates are often mild — warmer and moister than cold lands and cooler and breezier than hot lands. The weather may attract tourists, who bring income to the island.

But living on islands may have disadvantages, too. There may be a risk of flooding or of volcanic activity. It may be a challenge to keep in touch with the outside world. It is sometimes difficult to set up industries on islands. Consumer goods may be in short supply. Jobs are often scarce, and schooling may be hard to come by.

● Greenland is a very large island, but very few people live there. The island has an average of one person for every 15 square miles.

▼ Tristan da Cunha is one of several small islands in the South Atlantic Ocean.

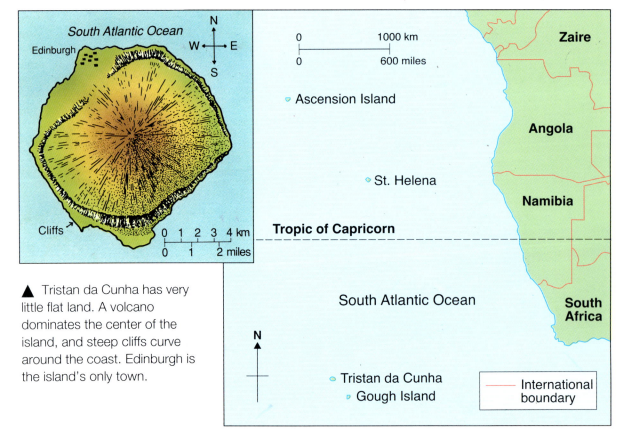

▲ Tristan da Cunha has very little flat land. A volcano dominates the center of the island, and steep cliffs curve around the coast. Edinburgh is the island's only town.

◀ Made in 1973, this special stamp from Tristan da Cunha commemorates the islanders' return in 1963.

Case Study

The British-owned island of Tristan da Cunha is among the loneliest inhabited places in the world. Located in the South Atlantic Ocean, 1,703 miles from southern Africa, this small island holds only a few hundred people. Tristan's volcano erupted in 1961. The islanders were taken to safety, or **evacuated**, to Britain, but they returned in 1963.

Farmers on Tristan raise cattle and pigs, and the chief crop is potatoes. The island depends on crawfish for its living and has a fish-processing and freezing plant. Tristan also earns money from its postage stamps, which collectors buy.

Tristan has been linked to the outside world by satellite telecommunications since 1992. A British naval vessel visits the island annually.

Geography Detective

Two hundred years ago, people who lived on remote islands kept in touch with the outside world by ship. Today many islands have radios, telephones, and computer links. Satellite dishes may pick up television pictures beamed from the mainland.

How do you think this might affect the islanders' traditional way of life? How do modern communications change life on an island?

◀ This is the only harbor for boats on Tristan da Cunha. The British naval vessel, RMS *St. Helena*, waits outside the harbor. Ships carry passengers and mail to the island once a year.

Islands and Global Warming

The average temperatures around the world went up by 0.7°F between 1900 and 1980. Some scientists believe that temperatures may continue to rise, perhaps by another 4°F. This rise in world temperatures is called **global warming**. The change may be the result of people polluting the air with gases that come from car exhaust pipes, factory chimneys, and forest fires. These gases form a layer around the earth that traps warm air and holds in harmful substances called pollutants.

What impact does global warming have on islands? Warmer temperatures could melt the ice around the North and the South Poles. This change would cause sea levels to rise. New islands might be formed as coastal lowlands were flooded. Some islands might be drowned. Islanders would have to move away, and the wildlife and plants would be destroyed. The animals and plants of the islands of the Arctic and the Antarctic are used to cold conditions. They might die out if their living conditions warmed up.

● Several different kinds of penguins — flightless birds that thrive in a very cold climate — live on the islands near Antarctica. As global temperatures rise, the living conditions for these animals may change, warming the frigid islands on which they make their homes.

◀ The Florida Keys are a chain of low-lying islands made from coral limestone. They lie in warm seas off the southeastern coast of the United States. If sea levels rise as a result of global warming, the Keys could completely disappear within the next 60 years.

Case Study

The Republic of the Maldives, an Indian Ocean nation, is made up of 1,196 low-lying islands. Only 203 of the islands are inhabited. Most of the islands lie less than 10 feet above sea level, so rising oceans due to global warming could bring disaster to Maldivians. In fact, the United Nations has warned that rising sea levels may mean that archipelagos like the Maldives may disappear from the map.

Most Maldivian houses sit only 7 feet above sea level. Crops are grown at heights of about 3 feet. Islanders rely on tourism to make money, but high seas even now flood the capital's Malé International Airport. A further rise in sea level could make the Maldives unfit for people to live on or visit.

◀ Baros is one of the inhabited islands of the Maldives.

Geography Detective

Islanders all over the world depend on supplies of fresh water to cook with, to drink, and to water crops. Some fresh water comes from local underground springs and wells. What would happen if, as result of global warming, more salty water seeped into island groundwater? What other problems could a rise in sea level mean for low-lying islands?

Mapwork

The map on the opposite page shows an imaginary island in the Atlantic Ocean. The island has a mild climate, with wet summers and cold winters. Its economy depends on tourism and on the mining of local rock.

1. Make a copy of the map to show the coastline, the rivers, and the mountain peaks. Draw in the features listed below using the symbols in the key.
   a) A fishing village with a harbor
   b) A small town where tourists can stay
   c) A main road linking the two settlements
   d) An airstrip where small aircraft can land
   e) A track leading from the above-ground mine, or quarry, to the small town
   f) A hotel
   g) Fields for growing vegetables.

2. Use the scale on the map to measure these distances:
   a) from the quarry to the mouth of the river on the west side of the island;
   b) from the northern tip to the southern tip of the island;
   c) from the fishing village to the small town;
   d) all around the coast of the island.

3. Use the compass on the map to work out in which direction you would travel:
   a) from the 3,000-foot mountain to the 2,500-foot mountain;
   b) from the 1,000-foot hill to the 2,500-foot mountain;
   c) from the quarry to the mouth of the river in the northwest of the island.

4. What do you think the stone from the quarry is used for?

5. Write a description of the island.

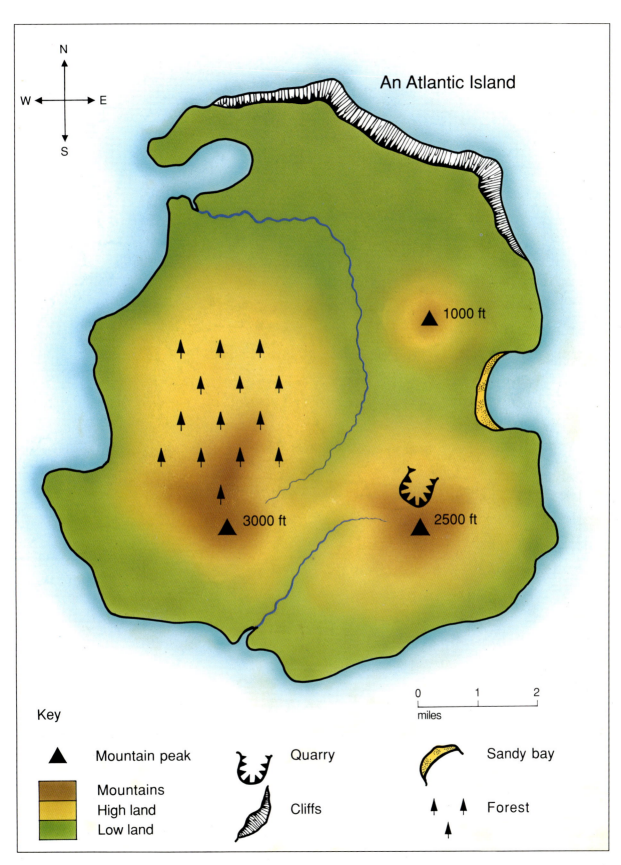

Glossary

accretion: A slow buildup or increase in size.

algae: Simple forms of plant life that grow in water.

archipelago: A group or chain of islands.

atoll: A ring-shaped coral island or archipelago.

caldera: A large crater left in a mountain after a volcanic eruption.

colonize: To settle or take over an area already inhabited by plants, animals, or humans.

continental shelf: The edge of a continent that lies below sea level. The sea above it is shallower than 1,000 feet.

coral: One of a group of small sea creatures whose hard, chalky casings build up into a coral reef.

crannog: An artificial island built in lakes in Ireland and Scotland about 2,000 years ago.

crust: The hard outer layer of rocks that makes up the earth.

delta: A fan-shaped deposit at the mouth of a river. It divides the river into many smaller channels. It is named after the triangular shape of the Greek letter delta Δ.

endangered: At risk of dying out.

erode: To wear down rock by the action of wind, water, ice, or weather.

evacuate: To take away to a safe place.

extinct: No longer living (of animals) or active (of volcanoes).

fossil: The remains of a prehistoric animal or plant that have been preserved in rock.

global warming: An increase in average world temperatures. Some scientists believe the trend is caused by burning forests and fuels such as coal and gasoline.

guano: Bird droppings that have collected and hardened into a thick mass. When refined, guano can be used as fertilizer.

headland: A piece of land sticking out into the sea.

ice age: A long cold period when ice sheets cover much of the earth. The last Ice Age ended about 10,000 years ago.

isthmus: A narrow neck of land joining a peninsula to the mainland.

lagoon: An area of shallow water separated from the open sea by reefs or sandbanks.

lava: The red-hot, liquid rock that is thrown out when a volcano erupts.

magma: Red-hot, liquid rock from deep inside the earth.

meander: A bend in the course of a river.

monsoon: A strong seasonal wind that brings heavy rain at the same time each year, primarily to Asian countries.

outcrop: A section of hard rock that sticks out at the earth's surface.

peninsula: Meaning "almost island," a piece of land that extends into the sea.

plate: One of the huge sections of the earth's crust that moves very slowly.

reef: A platform of rock or coral at or near the surface of the sea.

refuge: A safe place.

sea level: The surface of the sea from which the height of land is measured.

sediment: Mud, sand, broken shells, and stone that are carried along by water, then deposited.

stack: A small island that is formed when the sea erodes a headland.

volcano: A point on the earth's crust where gases and magma break through with explosive force.

METRIC CONVERSION CHART		
WHEN YOU KNOW	**MULTIPLY BY**	**TO FIND**
inches	25.4	millimeters
inches	2.54	centimeters
feet	0.3048	meters
miles	1.609	kilometers
square miles	2.59	square kilometers
acres	0.4047	hectares
gallons	3.78	liters
degrees Fahrenheit	.56 (after subtracting 32)	degrees Celsius

Index

Africa 22, 25
airports 19, 27
animals 9, 21, 22, 23, 26
Antarctica 5, 26
archipelagos 4, 5, 16, 27
Arctic 5, 22, 26
artificial islands 18, 19
atolls 16, 17
Australia 4, 7, 10, 17, 21

Bananal Island 10
birds 9, 20, 21, 22
Borneo 7
Brazil 9, 10
Britain 6, 19, 21

Canada 5, 11, 13
Caribbean Sea 23
Chincha Islands 9
continental shelves 12, 13
continents 4, 5, 12, 13
coral islands 16, 17
crannogs 18

deltas 8, 9
dunes 8

erosion 6, 7, 10

Finland 11
floods 7, 11, 19, 21, 26, 27
Florida Keys 26
fossils 13
France 5, 6
Fraser Island 4

Galápagos Islands 22, 23
global warming 26, 27
Greenland 5, 24
guano 9

Hawaiian Islands 14
Heimaey 15

Ice Age 6, 7, 11
Iceland 14, 15
Indian Ocean 21, 27
Indonesia 5, 21

isthmuses 4, 6

Japan 19
Java 7

Kilauea 14
Kodiak Island 23
Krakatoa 21
Kwajalein 17

lakes 5, 11, 15, 18, 19

Madagascar 21, 23
Malaita 19
Maldives 27
Manitoulin 11
meanders 10
Mexico 8, 18
Mont St. Michel 5
Moorea 17

Nauru 9
New Guinea 7
New Zealand 21
Newfoundland 13

Pacific Ocean 14, 17, 19, 22
peninsulas 4
plants 8, 20, 26
plates 12, 14
pollution 26

rivers 5, 10, 11

South Atlantic Ocean 24, 25
Spirit Island 5
stacks 6
Sumatra 7
Surtsey 14
Switzerland 18

Tasmania 4
Tristan da Cunha 24, 25

United States 6, 11, 15, 26

volcanoes 14, 15, 16, 21, 24

water supply 5, 27